Voting in America

Researching American History

introduced and edited by
JoAnne Weisman Deitch

A detail from the painting "Stump Speaking," by George Caleb Bingham, 1854. Rural politicking in mid-18th century America.

Discovery Enterprises, Ltd.
Carlisle, Massachusetts

First Edition © Discovery Enterprises, Ltd., Carlisle, MA 2003

ISBN: 1-57960-092-1

Library of Congress Catalog Card Number 2003101146

10 9 8 7 6 5 4 3 2 1

Printed in the United States of America

Subject Reference Guide:

Title: *Voting in America*
Series*: Researching American History*
introduced and edited by JoAnne Weisman Deitch

Credits:

Cover art: George Caleb Bingham's *The County Election*, 1851-52.

A polling place on the steps of the courthouse in Saline County, Missouri, in 1846. In this painting, we see the judge *(top center)* administering an oath to a voter. The voter is swearing, with his hand on the bible, that he is entitled to vote and has not already done so. There was no system of voter registration, so this oath and the possibility that the judge might recognize him if he came back was all that prevented a voter from voting again and again. Courtesy of the St. Louis Art Museum. Found at www.cs.uiowa.edu/-jones/voting/pictures

All other illustrations credited where they appear in the text.

Contents

About the Series

Researching American History is a series of books which introduces various topics and periods in our nation's history through the study of primary source documents.

Reading the Historical Documents

On the following pages you'll find words written by people during or soon after the time of the events. This is firsthand information about what life was like back then. Illustrations are also created to record history. These historical documents are called **primary source materials**.

At first, some things written in earlier times may seem difficult to understand. Language changes over the years, and the objects and activities described might be unfamiliar. Also, spellings were sometimes different. Below is a model which describes how we help with these challenges.

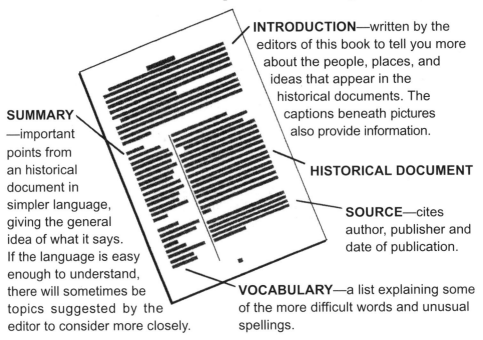

INTRODUCTION—written by the editors of this book to tell you more about the people, places, and ideas that appear in the historical documents. The captions beneath pictures also provide information.

SUMMARY—important points from an historical document in simpler language, giving the general idea of what it says. If the language is easy enough to understand, there will sometimes be topics suggested by the editor to consider more closely.

HISTORICAL DOCUMENT

SOURCE—cites author, publisher and date of publication.

VOCABULARY—a list explaining some of the more difficult words and unusual spellings.

In these historical documents, you may see three periods (…) called an ellipsis. It means that the editor has left out some words or sentences. You may see some words in brackets, such as [and]. These are words the editor has added to make the meaning clearer. When you use a document in a paper you're writing, you should include any ellipses and brackets it contains, just as you see them here. Be sure to give complete information about the author, title, and publisher of anything that was written by someone other than you.

Introduction

"Records of voting go back as long as there is written history. The ancient Greeks voted by acclamation or a clash of spears on shields. Other means of voting over the ages have included casting pebbles in urns, division of crowds into groups, or balloting with shells, disks or written ballots. In the original 13 colonies, voting was done by walking to an appointed local official and voice voting preference for all to hear. Secret balloting in the United States was first done in 1888 on a printed paper ballot. It was advanced a few years later by the voting machine." (Source: Sequoia Voting Systems)

"When the Founding Fathers established election guidelines at the Constitutional Convention in 1787, the process of electing a president differed greatly from what it is today. At that time, the right to vote belonged to some white males over the age of 21. It was not extended to women, Blacks, or Native Americans. Although Blacks won the right to vote when the 15th Amendment was ratified in 1870, it wasn't until 1965 that the Voting Rights Amendment was passed, assuring Blacks and other racial minorities the right to vote. Women were to fight for suffrage until 1919, when the 19th Amendment was passed. But voting laws were still not set as final. In 1971, the 26th Amendment reduced the national voting age to 18 from 21. The change was proposed in response to protests about the war in Vietnam. Young people argued 'If we're old enough to fight, we're old enough to vote.'

"The practice of national campaigns funded by well-defined political parties did not exist when the Founding Fathers discussed election procedures, and with the arrival of political parties, the whole method of campaigning for office was changed.

"During the Constitutional Convention, the major concern of electing a President for the country led to much debate. "A Committee of Eleven" in the Constitutional Convention proposed an indirect election of the president through a College of Electors. The first design of the Electoral College lasted through only four presidential elections. For in the meantime, political parties had emerged in the United States. The very people who had been condemning parties publicly had nevertheless been building them privately....

"One of the accidental results of the development of political parties was that in the presidential election of 1800, the Electors of the Democratic-

Republican Party gave Thomas Jefferson and Aaron Burr (both of that party) an equal number of electoral votes. The tie was resolved by the House of Representatives in Jefferson's favor—but only after 36 tries and some serious political dealings which were considered unseemly at the time. Since this sort of bargaining over the presidency was the very thing the Electoral College was supposed to prevent, the Congress and the States hastily adopted the Twelfth Amendment to the Constitution by September of 1804." (Source: Federal Election Commission (FEC)

Political Parties

"In order to avoid factions, the Constitution grants political parties no role in selecting a president. Ironically, political factions sprang up right away to support the Constitution and to oppose it. By the presidential election of 1796, political parties were firmly in place in America. The Federalists followed Secretary of the Treasury Alexander Hamilton. The Democratic-Republicans (also called the Jeffersonians) followed Thomas Jefferson and James Madison—the very James Madison who had earlier warned against factions. Today the party system seems firmly entrenched. Some Americans might argue that there is no real difference between the ideals and political stance of today's parties. Other Americans routinely vote a "party ticket" in their belief that a particular political party will best represent their wishes for governing the nation. In light of the role played by today's political parties, do you think our founding fathers' concerns about creating factions was warranted? Does our current party system give adequate voting choice to most Americans? What do you think the future might hold for America's party system?" (Source: Library of Congress, found at http://learning.loc.gov/learn/features/election/partysys.html)

The Election of Congress

Although the election of the President and Vice President generates the most interest among voters, the elections of Representatives and Senators are crucial to the functioning of our Federal government and to the process of making laws. In this book we will look at the qualifications for Congressmen and women and for Senators, and how they, once elected, cast their votes and pass bills into law.

Note: A Glossary of Voting and Election terms appears on pp. 49-51.

Electing the President

The Presidential Oath

"I do solemnly swear (or affirm) that I will faithfully execute the office of President of the United States, and will to the best of my ability, preserve, protect and defend the Constitution of the United States."

— United States Constitution, Article 11, Section 2, Clause 8

As originally drafted at the Constitutional Convention of 1787, the oath had even fewer than these 35 words. All the Committee of Detail wanted was that the President "faithfully execute" his office. Deeming this insufficient, George Mason and James Madison added the phrase about preserving the Constitution. Their amendment passed the committee by a vote of 7 to 1, with two members absent. (Source: *Constitution*, Vol. 5, No 1, NY: Winter 1993, p. 79)

The First Presidential Inauguration. GeorgeWashington takes the oath of office. (National Archives and Records Administration)

George Washington's concerns

"...In confidence I tell you (with the world it would obtain little credit) that my movements to the chair of government will be accompanied by feelings not unlike those of a culprit, who is going to the place of his execution; so unwilling am I, in the evening of a life nearly consumed in public cares, to quit a peaceful abode for an ocean of difficulties, without that competency of political skill, abilities, and inclination, which are necessary to manage the helm."

Consider this:

Describe in your own words how Washington felt about becoming president.

Source: George Washington's Letter to Henry Knox, 1788. Found in Joseph B. Bishop, *Our Political Drama: Conventions, Campaigns, Candidates*, NY: Scott-Thaw, 1904, p. 162.

A Home for the President

The nation's second president, John Adams, had served as Vice President under George Washington for eight years. Born in Quincy, Massachusetts, he first became well known when he defended the British Captain Thomas Preston, who had been charged with murder during the Boston Massacre. Although he was a true patriot, as a lawyer Adams believed that even a political enemy deserved a fair trial. When Adams' client was found not guilty of murder, Adams' reputation spread throughout the colonies. He participated in drafting the Declaration of Independence in 1776, and was elected to the presidency in 1797, as a Federalist. In 1800, John and his wife Abigail were the first occupants of the White House located in the new capital city of Washington. Since then, every U.S. president has lived at the White House during his term of office.

An early drawing of the White House, designed by James Hoban. The building cost $400,000, which was an enormous amount for that time. There were no stairs or bathrooms when John and Abigail Adams moved into the house. (Courtesy of the Maryland Historical Society)

An Unusual Election

John Quincy Adams, son of the second president, became the nation's sixth president in 1825. He was the only president ever elected who received fewer electoral votes and popular votes than an opponent in the election. Since no candidate had won a majority of electoral votes, the decision was turned over to the House of Representatives to choose a winner from the top three candidates of the four who ran. Although Andrew Jackson had received the highest electoral and popular vote count, Henry Clay turned his electoral votes over to Adams, who then was declared the winner.

Andrew Jackson, the father of modern party politics

"Andrew Jackson, the seventh president of the United States, from 1829 to 1837, helped to change both the nature of presidential elections and the character of the presidency.... He possessed a strict moral code and on many occasions resorted to duels to protect his honor. His nickname, "Old Hickory," likened him to the toughest American hardwood.

. . . .

"Between 1824 and 1828, Jackson and his associates worked at the grassroots level to build a popular-level opposition to Adams's administration. Average citizens became involved in politics in record numbers, as the Democrats organized local and state party conventions. The campaign of 1828 was one of the dirtiest in American history up to that point, in terms of back-stabbing and personal attacks. In the end, Jackson's appeal to the people paid off, when he was elected by a landslide.

"President Jackson's aggressive use of the veto – a power that other presidents had used only sparingly—set a precedent for a much stronger presidential role in national policy-making. He also contributed to shaping the country's elective process: His was America's first modern political party, and never again would a candidate win the White House without engaging in party politics and making a direct appeal to the American people." (Source: Elections and Voting Exhibit, National Museum of American History, Washington, DC: Smithsonian Institution)

Consider this:
Prior to the late 1820s, presidential elections saw little in the way of the candidates campaigning with graphics or songs. Jackson was one of the first to select music to enhance his campaign. He chose a march with patriotic appeal to project his image to the voters. What methods do today's candidates use to add spirit to their campaigns?

Chief Justice John Marshall administering the oath of office to Andrew Jackson on the east portico of the Capitol, March 4, 1829. This is a panel of the mural on the ceiling of the Capitol. (Courtesy of the Library of Congress)

Crowds in front of the White House headed to the open house to celebrate Jackson's inauguration. The rowdy group destroyed furniture and much of the decor.

Jackson's Victory Marked a New Era

Looking back on the first fifty years of presidential elections, historians can see considerable changes from the colonial period to Andrew Jackson's victory in 1829.

Political Development in the United States

Inauguration Day, 1829 was tumultuous. Thousands of people descended on the White House grounds to celebrate Andrew Jackson's decisive victory over John Quincy Adams, nearly injuring the new president in their fervor and doing some considerable damage to physical property. These frenetic events, which horrified some observers and delighted others, symbolized the culmination of a half century of American political development under the Constitution. Two political parties had vigorously contested for the highest office in the nation, more than one million voters in twenty-four states had cast ballots, and each candidate had received substantial support from devoted adherents. A man whom some considered violent, uncouth, and rustic, but whom others thought of as a tribune of the common people, had successfully challenged the leader of the eastern establishment.

Fifty years before, the political situation had not been as energetic, as organized, as large scale, or as complex. Colonial politics had had its share of political conflicts between vigorously contesting social groups, bitter political rhetoric, and sharp electoral confrontation. But relatively few people had been involved in these battles. In most colonies, laws severely restricted the number of citizens who could vote.

Source: *Political Ideology and Voting Behavior in the Age of Jackson,* Chpt 2, Joel H. Silbey; Prentice-Hall, Inc., 1973.

Summary:

Inauguration day was wild. Jackson had beaten John Quincy Adams by a big margin, and when the crowds came to the White House to celebrate, they did quite a bit of damage. More than 1 million people from 24 states had voted for their favored candidate from the two political parties. The winner represented the common man, rather than the "Eastern establishment."

During the Colonial period, few people had been allowed to vote, and there was not much energy involved in politics.

Vocabulary

adherent = supporter of a cause
culmination = climax
decisive = conclusive
fervor = intense emotion
frenetic = frantic
rhetoric = prose
rustic = typical of country life; simple
tribune = champion of the people
tumultuous = noisy
uncouth = crude

How the Federal Convention Dealt with Electing a President

Instead of having the people vote directly for the President and Vice President, an electoral system was set up to prevent corruption in counting votes.

Summary:
Members of the convention hoped that by having electors in each state cast votes the presidential election would be free of corruption.

Vocabulary:
apportioning = dividing
combination = an
  association for a
  common purpose
indulge = allow oneself
  the pleasure
intrigue = secret scheme
perpetual = lasting
  indefinitely

Records of the Federal Convention of 1787:

...[T]he members of the General Convention...did indulge the hope [that] by apportioning, limiting, and confining the Electors within their respective States, and by the guarded manner of giving and transmitting the ballots of the Electors to the Seat of Government, that intrigue, combination, and corruption, would be effectually shut out, and a free and pure election of the President of the United States made perpetual.

In the The Debates on the Adoption of the Federal Constitution, framers of the Constitution settled on what seems like a convoluted system to voters today:

Consider this:
Why do you suppose the electors were not allowed to be a member of the legislature?

Each state shall appoint, in such manner as its legislature may direct, a number of electors equal to the whole number of senators and members of the House of Representatives to which the state may be entitled in the legislature.

But no person shall be appointed an elector who is a member of the legislature of the United States, or who holds any office of profit or trust under the United States.

The 12th Amendment – 1804

The 12th Amendment to the Constitution made sure that electors would designate their votes for president and vice president. But, the 12th Amendment left in place a tie-breaking system by which the House of Representatives breaks a tie on presidential electoral votes and the Senate breaks a tie on vice presidential electoral votes.

Who Should be Allowed to Vote?

The founding fathers wrestled with the decision on who should be allowed to vote. James Madison described the problem this way:

The right of suffrage is a fundamental Article in Republican Constitutions. The regulation of it is, at the same time, a task of peculiar delicacy. Allow the right [to vote] exclusively to property [owners], and the rights of persons may be oppressed... . Extend it equally to all, and the rights of property [owners] ...may be overruled by a majority without property....

Vocabulary:

oppressed = persecuted

Eventually, framers of the Constitution left the vote question to the states. In Article I Section 4, the Constitution says:

The times, places and manner of holding elections for Senators and Representatives, shall be prescribed in each state by the legislature thereof; but the Congress may at any time by law make or alter such regulations... .

Unfortunately, leaving election control to individual states led to unfair voting practices in the U.S. At first, white men with property were the only Americans routinely permitted to vote. President Andrew Jackson, champion of frontiersmen, helped advance the political rights of those who did not own property.

By about 1860, most white men without property were enfranchised. But African Americans, women, Native Americans, non-English speakers and citizens between the ages of 18 and 21 had to fight for the right to vote in this country.

Another key issue was deciding upon the qualifications of those who could run for office. For national office, the following qualifications were to be met:

Consider this:
Did you know that our youngest president, John F. Kennedy, was 43 when elected, and the oldest, Ronald Reagan, was elected at 69 ?

• Candidates must be at least 35 year old.

• Candidates must be American citizens who were born in the United States. Naturalized citizens — those people who were born in foreign countries, but later attained U.S. citizenship — aren't eligible.

• Candidates must have lived in the United States for at least 14 years.

Constitutional Amendments Regarding Voting

There have been several Amendments to the U. S. Constitution which have altered or added to the text regarding voting and elections as framed by the founding fathers.

The 12th Amendment

"Under the 12th Amendment, each state's electors cast separate ballots for President and Vice-President. If no clear winner emerges, the House chooses the President from the top three competitors, and the Senate picks the Vice-President (its presiding officer) from the top two contenders. If the House remains deadlocked by Inauguration Day, the Vice-President assumes the presidency until the House resolves its deadlock....

"To this day, the people of the United States do not vote directly for the President and the Vice-President. Since 1804 senators and representatives have introduced hundreds of proposed amendments to rework or abolish the electoral college, and scholars have leveled a constant barrage of criticism against it—all to no avail. Every four years, the American people scratch their heads in puzzlement as they try to unravel its intricacies." (Source: Richard B. Bernstein, *CONSTITUTION*, Vol. 5 No. 1, Winter 1993, p. 48)

The Electors shall meet in their respective states, and vote by ballot for President and Vice-President ...; they shall name in their ballots the person voted for as President, and in distinct ballots, the person voted for as Vice-President, ...

Source: 12th Ammendment to the U.S. Constitution, ratified June 15, 1804.

Consider this:
Early paper ballots were slips of paper often provided by the voters themselves. Sometimes the political parties provided the ballots to the Electors of the Electoral College. Each ballot was for one office only (President or Vice President).

The Electoral College

In the United States, when people go to the polls to vote for President and Vice President, they are actually casting ballots for Electors. The electors then cast the votes that decide who becomes President.

In most presidential elections, the votes of the electors indicate the same winner as the popular vote count. Four times, however, the person who became the president did not receive the most popular votes (Rutherford Hayes, Benjamin Harrison, John Quincy Adams, and George W. Bush).

The founding fathers thought that using the electoral college would eliminate election problems, including the chance of corruption.

Vocabulary:

apportioning = to divide
   according to a plan;
   assign
intrigue = secret scheme
combination = association

...[T]he members of the General Convention...did indulge the hope [that] by apportioning, limiting, and confining the Electors within their respective States, and by the guarded manner of giving and transmitting the ballots of the Electors to the Seat of Government, that intrigue, combination, and corruption, would be effectually shut out, and a free and pure election of the President of the United States made perpetual.

Source: The Records of the Federal Convention of 1787.

The current workings of the Electoral College are the result of both design and experience. As it now operates:

Vocabulary:

allocated = set apart

- Each State is allocated a number of Electors equal to the number of its U.S. Senators (always 2) plus the number of its U.S. Representatives (which may change each decade according to the size of each State's population as determined in the Census).

- The political parties (or independent candidates) in each State submit to the State's chief election official a list of individuals pledged to their candidate for president and equal in

16

number to the State's electoral vote. Usually, the major political parties select these individuals either in their State party conventions or through appointment by their State party leaders while third parties and independent candidates merely designate theirs.

Note:
See question to consider on page 12.

- Members of Congress and employees of the federal government are prohibited from serving as an Elector in order to maintain the balance between the legislative and executive branches of the federal government.

- After their caucuses and primaries, the major parties nominate their candidates for president and vice president in their national conventions traditionally held in the summer preceding the election. (Third parties and independent candidates follow different procedures according to the individual State laws). The names of the duly nominated candidates are then officially submitted to each State's chief election official so that they might appear on the general election ballot.

- On the Tuesday following the first Monday of November in years divisible by four, the people in each State cast their ballots for the party slate of Electors representing their choice for president and vice president (although as a matter of practice, general election ballots normally say "Electors for" each set of candidates rather than list the individual Electors on each slate).

continued on next page

17

- Whichever party slate wins the most popular votes in the State becomes that State's Electors—so that, in effect, whichever presidential ticket gets the most popular votes in a State wins all the Electors of that State. [The two exceptions to this are Maine and Nebraska where two Electors are chosen by statewide popular vote and the remainder by the popular vote within each Congressional district].

- On the Monday following the second Wednesday of December (as established in federal law) each State's Electors meet in their respective State capitals and cast their electoral votes—one for president and one for vice president.

- In order to prevent Electors from voting only for "favorite sons" of their home State, at least one of their votes must be for a person from outside their State (though this is seldom a problem since the parties have consistently nominated presidential and vice presidential candidates from different States).

- The electoral votes are then sealed and transmitted from each State to the President of the Senate who, on the following January 6, opens and reads them before both houses of the Congress.

- The candidate for president with the most electoral votes, provided that it is an absolute majority (one over half of the total), is declared president. Similarly, the vice presidential candidate with the absolute majority of electoral votes is declared vice president.

- In the event no one obtains an absolute majority of electoral votes for president, the U.S. House of Representatives (as the chamber closest to the people) selects the president from among the top three contenders with each State casting only one vote and an absolute majority of the States being required to elect. Similarly, if no one obtains an absolute majority for vice president, then the U.S. Senate makes the selection from among the top two contenders for that office.

- At noon on January 20, the duly elected president and vice president are sworn into office.

Source: Found at http://www.fec.gov/pages/ecworks

Electoral College Box Scores

The National Archives and Records Administration provides a useful summary of all U.S. presidential elections on its web site. Following are the results of several of our national elections.

Consider this:
What does the [F] stand for?

Notes:
For all intents and purposes, Washington was unopposed for election as President. Under the system then in place, votes for Vice President were not differentiated from votes for President.

Notes:
Prior to ratification of the 12th Amendment, votes for President and Vice President were not listed on separate ballots. Although John Adams ran as Jefferson's main opponent in the general election, running-mates Jefferson and Burr received the same number of electoral votes. The election was decided in the House of Representatives, with 10 state delegations voting for Jefferson, 4 voting for Burr and 2 making no choice.

Election: 1789
President: George Washington [F]
Main Opponent: John Adams [F]
Electoral Vote: Winner: 69
Main Opponent: 34
Total/Majority: 69/35
Popular Vote: no record
Votes for Others: John Jay (9), Robert H. Harrison (6), John Rutledge (6), John Hancock (4), George Clinton (3), Samuel Huntington (2), John Milton (2), James Armstrong (1), Benjamin Lincoln (1), Edward Telfair (1)
Vice President: John Adams

Election: 1800
President: Thomas Jefferson [D-R]
Main Opponent: Aaron Burr [D-R]
Electoral Vote: Winner: 73
Main Opponent: 73
Total/Majority: 138/70
Popular Vote: no record
Votes for Others: John Adams (65), Charles C. Pinckney (64), John Jay (1)
Vice President: Aaron Burr

Election: 1836

President: Martin Van Buren [D]
Main Opponent: William Henry Harrison [W]
Electoral Vote: Winner: 170
Main Opponent: 73
Total/Majority: 294/148
Popular Vote: Winner: 762,678
Main Opponent: 735,651
Votes for Others: Hugh L. White (26),
Daniel Webster (14), William P. Mangum (11)
Vice President: Richard M. Johnson (147)
V.P. Opponents: Francis Granger (77),
John Tyler (47), William Smith (23)

Note:
The election for Vice President was decided in the Senate.

Election: 1876

President: Rutherford B. Hayes [R]
Main Opponent: Samuel J. Tilden [D]
Electoral Vote: Winner: 185
MainOpponent: 184
Total/Majority: 369/185
Popular Vote: Winner: 4,036,298
Main Opponent: 4,300,590
Vice President: William A. Wheeler (185)
V.P. Opponent: Thomas A. Henricks (184)

Note:
The electoral votes of 4 States were disputed. Congress referred the matter to the Electoral Commission which gave the decision to Rutherford B. Hayes.

Election: 1948

President: Harry S. Truman [D]
Main Opponent: Thomas E. Dewey [R]
Electoral Vote: Winner: 303
Main Opponent: 189
Total/Majority: 531/266
Popular Vote: Winner: 24,105,695
Main Opponent: 21,969,170
Votes for Others: J. Strom Thurmond (39)
Vice President: Alben W. Barkely (303)
V.P. Opponents: Earl Warren (189),
Fielding L. Wright (39)

Notes:
State's Rights Party candidate Thurmond received 1,169,021 popular votes for President. Progressive Party candidate Henry A. Wallace received 1,157,172 popular votes for President, but no electoral votes.

continued on next page

Note:

Vice Presidential candidate for the Democratic ticket was a woman, Geraldine Ferraro.

Note:

Independent candidate Ross Perot received 19,741,065 popular votes for President, but no electoral votes.

Election: 1984

President: Ronald Reagan [R]
Main Opponent: Walter F. Mondale [D]
Electoral Vote: Winner: 525
Main Opponent: 13
Total/Majority: 538/270
Popular Vote: Winner: 54,455,000
Main Opponent: 37,577,000
Vice President: George Bush (525)
V.P. Opponent: Geraldine A. Ferraro (13)

Election: 1992

President: William J. Clinton [D]
Main Opponent: George Bush [R]
Electoral Vote: Winner: 370
Main Opponent: 168
Total/Majority: 538/270
Popular Vote: Winner: 44,908,254
Main Opponent: 39,102,343
Vice President: Albert Gore, Jr. (370)
V.P. Opponent: James Danforth Quayle (168)

Source: Electoral College Box Scores, National Archives and Records Administration, found at www.archives. gov/federal_register/electoral_college

Negro Suffrage

Following the Civil War, blacks exercised their right to vote. In the South, and often elsewhere, the black voter had to deal with fraudulent vote-counting, and sometimes violence from those opposed to black suffrage.

Counting the Black Vote

In Southern Alabama, prominent leaders in democratic [party] politics said that in the "black districts" it was common to have, at each place of holding elections, two ballot-boxes, one for white voters, and the other for the Negroes.... If the blacks are present, and likely to vote in such numbers as to "threaten the overthrow of society," or give cause of alarm to leading white citizens, the offered vote of some ignorant Negro is challenged. The gangway is filled behind him by a long line of Negroes, pressing forward in single file, and impatient to vote. The Negro selected to be challenged is always one who lives in a distant part of the township or district. Somebody is dispatched to summon witnesses from his neighborhood, or some other cause of delay is discovered.... Of course the other Negroes cannot vote until this case is decided. It comes to an end by and by, and the conclusion which is at last reached is, usually, that the challenged Negro has the right to vote, and his ballot is accepted....When the hour for the closing of the polls arrives there has not been sufficient time for the full Negro republican [party] vote to be polled....

"But," I often inquired, "what if the Negroes should become tired of this enforced waiting, and, understanding its purpose, should push forward, and demand that their votes shall be received?"

continued on next page

Consider this:
Although some whites approved of the negro's right to vote, they were afraid that the black vote would change society. What specific changes might have worried them the most?

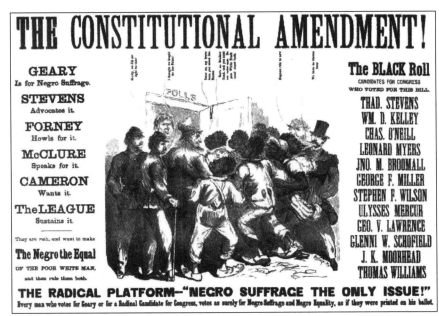

This poster was part of the campaign for the Democratic candidate for Governor of Pennsylvania in 1866 (Heister Clymer). It shows Blacks crowding Whites out in their rush to get into the polls. The Republican candidate was John White Geary, who favored Black suffrage. Issues such as suffrage were common campaign themes in national and state elections. (Courtesy of the Library of Congress)

Consider this:

List a few of the methods mentioned here that were used by whites to prevent the negro vote from being counted fairly.

"Then," answered my informants, significantly, "there is a collision. The, Negroes are the attacking party, and of course they will be worsted...."

In Southern Alabama and in Mississippi influential and prominent Democrats said to me: "Some of our people, some editors especially, deny that the Negroes are hindered from voting; but what is the good of lying? They *are* interfered with, and we are obliged to do it, and we may as well tell the truth."

Source: J.B. Harrison, "Studies in the South," *Atlantic Monthly* 50 (July 1882) pp.104. Found in William Loren Katz, *Eyewitness: A Living Documentary of the African American Contribution to American History,* NY: Simon & Schuster, 1995, pp. 311-12.

The 15th Amendment

In 1870, the 15th Amendment guaranteed the right to vote to all men that were 21 or older, regardless of race or ethnic background. In 1878, an act to amend the Constitution to grant women the right to vote was introduced into Congress. It took forty two years for legislators to adopt the amendment and obtain ratification by the states.

National Anti-Slavery Standard.

WITHOUT CONCEALMENT—WITHOUT COMPROMISE.

NEW YORK, SATURDAY, JULY 22, 1865.

PROPOSED AMENDMENT OF THE UNITED STATES CONSTITUTION.

No STATE SHALL MAKE ANY DISTINCTION IN CIVIL RIGHTS AND PRIVILEGES AMONG THE NATURALIZED CITIZENS OF THE UNITED STATES RESIDING WITHIN ITS LIMITS, OR AMONG PERSONS BORN ON ITS SOIL OF PARENTS PERMANENTLY RESIDENT THERE, ON AC-COUNT OF RACE, COLOR, OR DESCENT.

Wendell Phillips' antidiscrimination amendment ran in 1865-66 in the American Anti-Slavery Society's newspaper. This poster is pro-Black suffrage.

Woman's Suffrage

The long struggle for woman's suffrage spanned several generations and involved women of all ages. Many of the early leaders, like Elizabeth Cady Stanton, Lucretia Mott, Lucy Stone, and Susan B. Anthony, had been involved with abolitionist movements. None of the early leaders would live to see the 19th Amendment pass. In the later years there were younger, college-educated women who took up the challenge: women like Carrie Chapman Catt, a master at organization, and Alice Paul, who had learned her political tactics from the more militant women of England.

They held meetings, wrote articles, demonstrated, picketed, and paraded, until finally on August 26, 1920, woman's suffrage was signed into law. Following, an article from the *New York Times* describes one of the bigger parades for woman's suffrage held in New York.

Consider this:

How would you explain the men's attitude about the woman's suffrage movement, according to this reporter?

The Uprising of the Women

The parade on Fifth Avenue last evening of possibly 10,000 women of various ages, many of them young and personable, all surely representative of good types of womanhood. ...will be discussed from various points of view. Most of the comment it provokes will be humorous but amiable. Men generally view the woman suffrage movement calmly, seeming not to care much whether or not the women get the right to vote, and heeding little the consequences of the social revolution which would result from the triumph of the present agitation....

The situation is dangerous. We often hear the remark nowadays that women will get the vote if they try hard enough and persistently, and it is true that they will get it, and play havoc with it for themselves and society. ...if the men are not firm and wise enough and, it may as well be said, masculine enough to prevent them.

...Granted the suffrage, they would demand all that the right implies. It is not possible to think of women as soldiers and sailors, police patrolmen, or firemen, although voters ought to fight if need be, but they would serve on juries and elect themselves if they could to executive offices and judgeships. Many of them are looking forward to an apportionment of high offices between the sexes. This may seem preposterous to some of the men who choose to smile complacently at the aggressiveness of the women's rights adherents, but it is true. It is a state of things these men will have to cope with before they die if they do not arouse themselves and do their duty now....

In her pursuit of all the privileges and duties of men, however, she is deliberately endangering many rights she now enjoys....

It will be a sad day for society when woman loses the respect she now receives from all but the basest of men. Yet yesterday's parade demonstrates that she holds male courtesy in slight regard, or would, if we were willing to regard the parade as a demonstration of the feelings and opinions of all our women.

Millions of men labor all their years to keep up a home, of which a woman is mistress. But with the opportunity afforded to him by the refusal of woman to recognize his manhood as a title of supremacy in the world's affairs, he will be at pains to avoid some of the troubles which he has hitherto regarded as part of his heritage.

...There were, at most, 10,000 women in yesterday's parade. If their cause triumphs there will be 700,000 women voters in this municipality. Have the 10,000 thought much about the measure of influence they would exert if the whole number voted under the control of their associations and environment and as their intelligence impelled them to?

Source: The *New York Times*, May 5, 1912, p. 14.

Vocabulary:
adherents = supporters
basest = lowest
complacency = feeling of
    satisfaction
hitherto = until this time
impelled = pressured

The 19th Amendment

Consider this:
During World War I, militant suffragists, demanding that President Wilson reverse his opposition to a federal amendment, stood vigil at the White House and carried banners such as this one comparing the President to Kaiser Wilhelm II of Germany. In the heated patriotic climate of wartime, such tactics met with hostility and sometimes violence and arrests.

(National Archives and Records Administration)

Consider this:
Women are still working for equal rights in other areas. Explain.

Vocabulary:
abridged = cut short

The right of citizens of the United States to vote shall not be denied or abridged by the United States or by any state on account of sex.

Source: 19th Amendment to the U. S. Constitution.

"From the very beginning, the inequality of men and women under the Constitution has been an issue for advocacy...." Woman's Suffrage was passed, but the work was not yet complete for equal rights for women. As Alice Paul pointed out in 1923, at the 75th anniversary of the 1848 Seneca Falls Conference: "We shall not be safe until the principle of equal rights is written into the framework of our government." (Source: *Equal Rights Amendment* by Roberta W. Francis, Chair, ERA Task Force, National Council of Women's Organizations, found at www.equalrightsamendment.org/era)

The Equal Rights Amendment

"WELL, GIRLS, AT LEAST THE ONLY WAY WE CAN GO IS UP."

"Freedom from legal sex discrimination, Alice Paul believed, required an Equal Rights Amendment that affirmed the equal application of the Constitution to all citizens. In 1923,... she introduced the "Lucretia Mott Amendment," which read: "Men and women shall have equal rights throughout the United States and every place subject to its jurisdiction." The amendment was introduced in every session of Congress until it passed in 1972....

"The Equal Rights Amendment was reintroduced in Congress on July 14, 1982 and has been before every session of Congress since that time. In the 107th Congress (2001 - 2002), it has been introduced as S.J.Res. 10 (chief sponsor: Sen. Edward Kennedy, MA) and H.J.Res. 40 (chief sponsor: Rep. Carolyn Maloney, NY). These bills impose no deadline on the ERA ratification process. Success in putting the ERA into the Constitution via this process would require passage by a two-thirds in each house of Congress and ratification by 38 states."

Source: *Equal Rights Amendment* by Roberta W. Francis, Chair, ERA Task Force, National Council of Women's Organizations, found at www.equalrightsamendment.org/era.

The Things that Qualify
a Colored Man to Vote
in the Southern States

IN order that you may know what will be demanded of you to vote under the Constitutions and laws of the several Southern States, we give below the substantial requirements of each, to wit :—

IN Alabama, Louisiana, Mississippi, North Carolina, South Carolina, Virginia and Tennessee

YOU MUST PAY YOUR POLL TAX.

YOU MUST REGISTER AND HOLD YOUR CERTIFICATE OF REGISTRATION.

If you can read and write you can register.

IN Alabama, Louisiana and South Carolina

If you cannot read and write you can register if you own $300 worth of property.

IN Arkansas and Georgia

YOU MUST PAY YOUR POLL TAX.

IN Florida, Kentucky, Texas and West Virginia

You must reside in the State.

A man convicted of almost any crime may be barred from voting.

Although Blacks had been given the right to vote, many states, especially in the South, imposed poll taxes, preventing most poor people from voting. This page, reproduced from a pamphlet entitled To the colored men of voting age in the southern states, *lists the rules in some of those states. Note the reference to owning property in Alabama, Louisiana, and South Carolina.* (Source: Courtesy of the Library of Congress, found at http://memory.loc.gov/cgi-bin/ampage)

The 24th Amendment

At the ceremony in 1964 formalizing the 24th Amendment, President Lyndon Johnson stated "There can be no one too poor to vote." (July 2, 1964 photo by Cecil Stoughton, LBJ Library) *Do you recognize anyone else in the photo? In 1965 The Voting Rights Act was amended to ban the use of literacy tests, poll taxes, and other barriers to voting.*

Many Southern states adopted a poll tax in the late 1800s, limiting the ability of poor people, of any race, to vote. Although former slaves had been given the right to vote by the 15th Amendment, many did not have the money to pay a poll tax. Others could not vote because of the difficult literacy tests.

Section 1. The right of citizens of the United States to vote in any primary or other election for President or Vice President, for electors for President or Vice President, or for Senator or Representative in Congress, shall not be denied or abridged by the United States or any state by reason of failure to pay any poll tax or other tax.

Source: 24th Amendment to the U. S. Constitution.

Literacy Test

I, _____, do hereby apply to the Board of Registrars of _____County, State of Alabama, to register as an elector under the Constitution and laws of the State of Alabama, and do herewith submit answers to the interrogatories propounded to me by said Board.

_____
(Applicants Full Names)

QUESTIONNAIRE

1. State your name, the date and place of your birth, and your present address.
_____

_____

2. Are you single or married?_____(a)   If married, give name, resident and place of birth of your husband or wife, as the case may be:_____

_____

3. Give the names of the places, respectively, where you have lived during the last five years; and the name or names by which you have been known during the last five years:
_____

_____

4.   If you are self-employed, state the nature of your business:_____

_____

5. If you claim that you are a bona fide resident of the state of Alabama, give the date on which you claim to have become such bona fide resident: _____(a) When did you become a bona fide resident of _____County? _____(b)   When did you become a bona fide resident of Ward or Precinct? _____

6. If you intend to change your place of residence prior to the next general election, state the facts:_____

_____

7. Have you previously applied for and been denied registration as a voter?
_____
If so give the facts:_____

_____

8. Has your name been previously stricken from the list of persons

First page of a 3-page voter literacy test from Alabama prevented many uneducated Blacks and Whites from voting. Such tests were finally abolished in the 1960s. (Source: Found at www.voterights.org/literacy.html)

The 26th Amendment

The Vietnam War aroused young men of draft age to demonstrate for changing the voting age to 18 from 21. Young adults and others felt that they were old enough to vote if they were old enough to risk their lives for their country. This illustration, encouraging young Americans to register to vote is a detail from a poster published by Glencoe McGraw-Hill entitled "The Constitution and You - 26th Amendment."

In the 1960s, young people in America became politically active when the war in Vietnam made them realize that their best way to speak out about their attitudes was to vote. As a result of the 26th Amendment to the Constitution, the voting age was lowered to 18.

Section 1. The right of citizens of the United States, who are 18 years of age or older, to vote, shall not be denied or abridged by the United States or any state on account of age.

Source: 26th Amendment to the U. S. Constitution.

Consider this:
How would you feel if you could be drafted into the U. S. Armed Services, but not allowed to vote because of your age?

Methods of Voting

Methods of voting in America ranged from a voice vote, to paper ballots which were hand-counted, to levers pulled in voting booths with curtains for privacy. The latest technology uses "ATM-like voting machine[s] that would allow the voter to choose an English or Spanish ballot.

"Like an ATM machine, the voter first sticks a card into a slot and selects the language in which he wants to vote. Then, on a computer monitor, the voter touches the names of candidates for whom he wants to vote.

"The machine prevents overvoting or voting for too many candidates in a race." (Source: Sequoia Voting Systems)

Voting by voicing preference. (Detail from cover)

Suffragists vote by paper ballot.

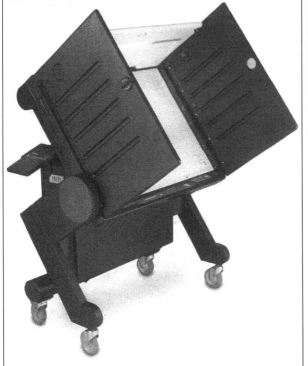

Example of a modern touch-screen computerized voting machine from Sequoia Voting Systems.

Voting booth with levers, used in the 1930s to 1980s.

Electing Congress

Article I

Section 1. All legislative powers herein granted shall be vested in a Congress of the United States, which shall consist of a Senate and House of Representatives.

Section 2. The House of Representatives shall be composed of members chosen every second year by the people of the several states, and the electors in each state shall have the qualifications requisite for electors of the most numerous branch of the state legislature.

No person shall be a Representative who shall not have attained to the age of twenty five years, and been seven years a citizen of the United States, and who shall not, when elected, be an inhabitant of that state in which he shall be chosen.

Representatives and direct taxes shall be apportioned among the several states which may be included within this union, according to their respective numbers, which shall be determined by adding to the whole number of free persons, including those bound to service for a term of years, and excluding Indians not taxed, three fifths of all other Persons. The actual Enumeration shall be made within three years after the first meeting of the Congress of the United States, and within every subsequent term of ten years, in such manner as they shall by law direct. The number of Representatives shall not exceed one for every thirty thousand, but each state shall have at least one Representative; and until such enumeration shall be made, the state of New Hampshire shall be entitled to chuse three, Massachusetts eight,

continued on next page

Vocabulary:
requisite = required
vested = placed in the
  control of

Consider this:
Many Indians were not taxed, so they were not counted. It was not until 1947 that Indians were enfranchised. (See page 50, top activity)

Vocabulary:

writs of election = an
   order by a governor or
   other executive that a
   special election be held

Rhode Island and Providence Plantations one, Connecticut five, New York six, New Jersey four, Pennsylvania eight, Delaware one, Maryland six, Virginia ten, North Carolina five, South Carolina five, and Georgia three.

When vacancies happen in the Representation from any state, the executive authority thereof shall issue writs of election to fill such vacancies.

The House of Representatives shall choose their speaker and other officers; and shall have the sole power of impeachment.

Section 3. The Senate of the United States shall be composed of two Senators from each state, chosen by the legislature thereof, for six years; and each Senator shall have one vote.

The 17th Amendment - 1913

Things to do:

List the current Senators from your state, their political parties, and how long they have been in office.

The Senate of the United States shall be composed of two Senators from each state, elected by the people thereof, for six years; and each Senator shall have one vote. The electors in each state shall have the qualifications requisite for electors of the most numerous branch of the state legislatures.

When vacancies happen in the representation of any state in the Senate, the executive authority of such state shall issue writs of election to fill such vacancies: Provided, that the legislature of any state may empower the executive there-of to make temporary appointments until the people fill the vacancies by election as the legislature may direct.

This amendment shall not be so construed as to affect the election or term of any Senator chosen before it becomes valid as part of the Constitution.

Roll Call Voting

Members of Congress vote in the House of Representatives and in the Senate. Because they have to answer to their constituents, they have roll call votes, instead of secret ballots. During the 200 years since our Constitution, there have been millions of roll call votes. Even when Congressional votes decide certain issues, the President still has veto power.

What goes on in Congress today

...Congress both considers a wide variety of substantive issues and represents the diverse constituencies of 435 congressional districts and 50 states....

Expressions such as "liberal," "moderate," and "conservative" are part of the common language used to denote the political orientation of a member of Congress; such labels are useful because they furnish a rough guide to the positions a politician is likely to take on a wide variety of issues. A contemporary liberal, for example, is likely to support an increase in the minimum wage; oppose a reduction in the capital gains tax; oppose the use of military force abroad; oppose further funds for Star Wars; support mandatory affirmative action programs; and support federal funding of health care and day care programs. Indeed, just knowing that a politician opposes increasing the minimum wage is enough information to predict, with a fair degree of reliability, the politician's views on many seemingly unrelated issues.

Source: *Congress: A Political-Economic History of Roll Call Voting,* by Keith T. Poole, Howard Rosenthal; Oxford University Press, 1997.

Vocabulary:

capital gains tax = tax on the profit from the sale of an asset

constituents = people who live within the areas that elected officials represent

denote = signify

mandatory = required; mandated

orientation = position

substantive = real

Consider this:

Why do constituents have the right to know how their representatives and senators vote on an issue?

Things to do:

Choose a senator or representative and write a profile of his or her political orientation based on current issues.

Frequently Asked Questions about Congress

There have been many books from the Government Printing Office that answer questions about how our government works. One of the most useful is entitled *The Capitol: Symbol of Freedom.* An excerpt follows.

Consider this:

Do you know who your Representatives and Senators are?

What issues might arise when Congressional districts are being determined? Site an example from recent history. (Hint: There was quite a bit of controversy in redistricting issues in California in recent years.)

Vocabulary:

decennial = every ten years

How are Representatives elected?

Representatives are elected by direct vote of the people. This method has remained unchanged since the Constitution went into effect in 1789. If, because of death or resignation, a vacancy occurs in the House of Representatives, it can be filled only by a special election or at the next general election. The entire membership of the House of Representatives is up for election every 2 years.

How are Senators elected?

Since the adoption of the 17th Amendment to the Constitution, in effect for the first time for the election of 1914, Senators have been elected directly by the people. Prior to that time, Senators were elected by their State legislatures. If a vacancy occurs in the Senate, it is either filled by special election, or (in most States) may be filled by temporary appointment by the Governor.

What is a congressional district?

A congressional district is that area within a State that is represented by a Congressman in the House of Representatives. The number of Representatives to which each State is entitled is determined by Congress, but each State sets the boundaries and determines the geographical composition of its own districts.

What is the basis for setting up congressional districts?

Representatives are apportioned among the States on the basis of the population as determined by each decennial census. By the Constitution, each State is entitled to at least one

Representative, and each congressional district must have a population of at least 30,000....all congressional districts should contain the same number of people, but shifting population, geographical complications, and other factors make this impossible....

Must a Representative reside within the district that he represents?

No. The Constitution merely states that a Representative "when elected, be an inhabitant of that State in which he shall be chosen." However, for practical purposes it is considered politically indispensable for a candidate to be a legal resident of the district he hopes to represent.

May the President ever preside over sessions of Congress?

No. This would be a violation of the separation of powers among the leistative, executive, and judicial branches. Whenever the President appears in Congress he does so as a guest.

What is the procedure in case of a dispute over the election of a candidate to the House of Representatives?

The Constitution says: "Each House shall be the judge of the elections, returns, and qualifications of its own Members." This means that if a congressional election is contested, a committee of the House of Representatives investigates the election and makes recommendations which are usually followed by the House.

What is meant by the term "Congressman at large"?

A Congressman at large is a Member of the House of Representatives who has been elected by the voters of an entire State rather than by those in a specific congressional district.

continued on next page

Consider this:
What might "geographical complications" refer to?

Vocabulary:
indispensable = essential

Consider this:

If you had to choose a committee to participate on, which committee would it be?

What issues would you want to bring up for discussion?

Both the House of Representatives and the Senate have fairly elaborate systems of committees. What form do these committees normally take?

Congressional committees may be classified in four main groups: (1) standing or permanent committees that continue from Congress to Congress, (2) special or select committees created on a temporary basis for a particular purpose, (3) joint standing committees composed of Members of both Houses, and (4) joint conference committees which work out differences between the two Houses on a particular bill. Standing committees divide themselves into subcommittees for the purpose of expediting their work. The House of Representatives has 20 standing committees, and the Senate 16 standing committees, which are as follows:

House of Representatives

Agriculture

Appropriations

Armed Services

Banking and Currency

District of Columbia

Education and Labor

Foreign Affairs

Government Operations

House Administration

Interior and Insular Affairs

Interstate and Foreign Commerce

Judiciary

Merchant Marine and Fisheries

Post Office and Civil Service

Public Works

Rules

Senate

Aeronautical and Space Sciences
Agriculture and Forestry
Appropriations
Armed Services
Banking and Currency
District of Columbia
Finance
Foreign Relations
Government Operations
Interior and Insular Affairs
Interstate and Foreign Commerce
Judiciary
Labor and Public Welfare
Post Office and Civil Service
Public Works
Rules and Administration

Things to do:
Choose one of the committees listed here from the House or Senate, and find out what they are involved with at this time.

Source: *The Capitol: Symbol of Freedom, House of Representatives of the United States, An Omnibus of the Capitol,* Fourth Edition, 89th Congress, House Document No. 260, p. 117.

2002 Enron Hearings in Senate Committee (Source: found at http://www.senate. gov/galleries/photo/gallery.htm)

How a Bill Becomes a Law

Introducing and passing legislation is an important function of both the House and the Senate. New proposals for laws (called bills before they become law) are assigned numbers, are studied and reported on by committees, and eventually based on the committee recommendations, are voted on.

Finally, if passed, the president signs them into law.

Summary of graphic:
A Congressman introduces a bill in the House of Representatives. The Speaker of the House refers the bill to the appropriate committee.

How a Law is Passed: From Conception to the Floor

Preparing and passing legislation (laws) is one of the more important duties of Congress. Here is a step-by-step discussion of how a bill is passed into law.

(1) Legislation in introduced: Anyone can propose a bill, but only a member of Congress can sponsor a bill. In the House of Representatives, the proposed legislation is handed to the clerk of the House, or placed in the hopper (a special box on the clerk's desk). In the Senate, the member proposing the legislation must gain recognition by the presiding officer or announce the proposed bill during the morning hour.

(2) The new bill (proposed legislation) is assigned a number that identifies it. It is labeled with the name of the sponsor or cosponsors (person or persons who proposed it), and copies are made and sent to committees.

(3) The committee in the House or Senate reviews the bill when it comes up on their calendar. The bill may be divided up into different parts that are sent to different committees or subcommittees, where hearings may be held, studies made, and findings are finally reported on to the committee. After this, a vote is made (order

to be reported) by the committee. If the committee does not review the bill, it is effectively killed at this point.

(4) After the vote, the committee may make revisions or amendments to the bill. If the bill is changed quite a bit by the amendments, the committee can ask that the bill be reintroduced again, including the changes.

(5) After the committee votes on the bill, they then prepare a document that explains why they favor passage of the bill. If a committee member in the minority opposes the bill, he or she can write a dissenting opinion.

(6) The bill is the placed on a calendar, where it will go before the floor. In the House of Representatives, the bill first goes to the Rules committee (unless they are bypassed by a special vote or procedure) who decides which rules will govern how the bill will be considered (time limits on the debate over the bill, for example, or forbidding the introduction of amendments).

(7) The bill then goes onto the House calendar (House of Representatives) or the Legislative calendar (Senate) to be discussed. The Speaker of the House and the majority leader decide when the bill will go to the floor in the House; a majority vote in the Senate can bring any bill to the floor. At this point, the bill is debated by the house of Congress it was introduced in. Supporters of the bill and detractors are both given equal time to discuss the bill. In the House of Representatives, the amount of time the bill can be debated is limited by the rules

Summary of graphic:
The Committee conducts hearings, then drafts a report and the necessary legislation, and submits it to the House.

Summary of graphic:
The House debates and passes the bill and forwards it to the Senate.

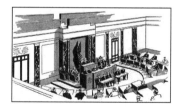

Summary of graphic:
The Senate refers the bill to its committee, debates it, then passes it, paralleling the House bill.

continued on next page

Summary of graphic:
The bill goes to the White House for the President's signature, and becomes law.

Summary of graphic:
Depending upon the nature of the bill, the Government is now equipped to deal with the problem it sought to solve. In the end the idea that became law seeks to do for the American people what the preamble of their constitution says it should do: "To form a more perfect Union, establish Justice, insure domestic Tranquility, provide for the common defense, promote the general Welfare, and secure the Blessings of Liberty to ourselves and our Posterity . . . "
. . .In any event, the result is to implement the will of the people!

committee, but in the Senate, the debate is unlimited unless cloture is invoked by a vote of 60 members. And in the Senate, some bills are defeated by "filibuster" or using up hours of debate time which effectively "kill" the bill unless cloture is voted.

(8) Finally, the bill is voted on by the House (which needs at least 218 members, or a quorum to vote) or the Senate. If the bill is passed, it is then sent to the other house of Congress. If either the House or the Senate do not pass the bill, then it dies. If both pass the bill, then it is sent to the President for signing. If the bill is changed a lot before passage in either the House or the Senate, then it is given to a Conference Committee. The conference committee is composed of members from both houses of Congress who work together to resolve differences. Once a compromise is reached, the bill is reintroduced to both houses and voted on.

(9) The President must sign the bill within ten days for it to become law. If the President vetoes the bill, it is sent back to Congress with the reasons why it wasn't signed. Both houses of congress can override the veto by a 2/3 majority vote.

(10) Once it is signed by the President, or the veto is overridden, then the bill becomes a law.

Source of text: Rapid Immigration.com, *Lesson One:The Legislative Branch: Making Laws to Protect Us*, found at http://www.rapidimmigration.com/usa/1

Source of Illustrations and Summary of Graphics: *The Capitol: Symbol of Freedom,* 89th Congress, 1st Session, H. Con. Res. 364, House Document No. 260, *How a Bill Becomes a Law,* p. 88.

Exercising Your Right to Vote

The Right to Vote: Electing your Government

Voting is one of the most important responsibilities of citizenship, and one of our most precious rights under the Constitution. By the process of voting, each individual has a say in who represents them, whether at the local level, the state level, or the federal level. This is known as the "consent of the governed" when with your vote, you say yes or no to policy makers.

Every Vote Counts

One of the problems confronting our nation in recent years has been the lack of voter turn-out on election days. This may occur because people don't realize how important even one vote can be: presidential elections have been won and lost by one vote in the past (President Andrew Johnson). And in 1776, only one vote determined that the English language would be the language of our country, instead of German.

Who is eligible to vote? In the United States, you must be a citizen, and at least eighteen years old to vote. You cannot be in prison, or on parole for a felony conviction, and must be deemed mentally competent. You must have been a resident of a precinct at least 30 days before the election, and you must be registered to vote at least 29 days before the election. If you meet these criteria, then you can vote in any election: local, state, or federal. This means you can have a say in who the next president and vice president of our country is; who your representatives in Congress will be, or who will sit on your local school board. You can also vote in primaries, which are special elections which help determine who the candidates for a political party will be.

Things to do:

List 5 important reasons for registering to vote. If you know a U. S. citizen of voting age who doesn't exercise his or her right to vote, encourage that person to vote, using what you have learned in this book.

Voter registration

In order for a citizen to vote in the U. S., he or she must first register.

Voter registration can be done by picking up an application that is usually available at places such as a local driver's licensing office, a post office, library, public assistance agency, office of the county commissioner of registration, or a county clerk's office. Once you are registered you can vote either at a polling booth in person, or by absentee ballot (which is mailed in early). You can also register as part of a political party when you register to vote. Normally, registration to vote is permanent, but you must re-register if you change your name (such as by marriage) or if you move and change your residence.

When the time comes to vote, you will normally go to a poll which is a special place located in your precinct (the voting area you live in). When you get to the poll, you will be given privacy while you vote. At the poll, there may be one of several methods used for voting. (See Voting Methods in the glossary, and p. 34.)

It is important before you go in to vote to ask any questions that you have about how to use the system your area has for voting (opening the curtain or leaving the booth will record the vote as final). Often there will be a "model" poll set up to practice with, and people manning the polls who will be happy to answer any questions.

Source: Rapid Immigration.com, *Lesson Nine: Learning How Citizenship Works for You.* Found at http://www.rapidimmigration.com/usa/

Voting is one of the most important rights granted to U. S. citizens. Now that you have learned something about the history of voting in America, you can see for yourself the great civic responsibility that our Founding Fathers and others in later years gave to Americans in the Constitution and in several constitutional amendments.

Glossary of Voting and Elections

Absentee Voting: A method of voting which enables registered voters to vote in a given election without physically going to the polls.

Bill: A proposal for a law, before it becomes law.

Campaign: A schedule of planned actions and events leading to the election of the candidate.

Candidate: An individual running for office in an election.

Caucus: Meetings where party members gather together to nominate a candidate. Caucuses usually involve a series of meetings held over weeks or months, attended by a select group of party members. Both the Democratic and Republican parties have their own rules governing caucuses and operation of the caucuses changes from state to state.

Citizen: A member of a state or other political community. Only United States citizens are allowed to vote in political elections.

Cloture: The procedure by which a debate is ended and a vote is taken.

Constituents: People who live within the areas that elected officials represent.

Delegate: An individual that is appointed or elected to represent others.

Democracy: A government of the people, by the people, and for the people.

Election Day: Federal elections are held on the first Tuesday, after the first Monday in November on even-numbered years. Presidential elections are held every four years. It is on this date that the American public votes for its choice of president.

Electoral College: The group of individuals who formally elect the United States president and vice-president.

Enfranchise: To endow with the right to vote.

Federal Election Commission (F.E.C.): A commission that oversees federal campaigns, founded in 1974.

G.O.P.: The Republican party, previously known as the **G**rand **O**ld **P**arty.

Grassroots: A grassroots campaign is one that involves the citizens (common people) as a main political group.

Incumbent: An individual currently holding a position of office. The incumbent president currently holds the office of president.

Independent: A voter who does not claim to be a member of a political party. (This voter will exercise a free choice in voting with either party on different candidates and issues.)

Issues: Ideas and points of debate that distinguish candidates in an election.

Landslide: The occurrence of a sweeping electoral victory, in which one candidate's votes far surpass those of other candidates.

Matching Funds: Primary presidential candidates are eligible to receive dollar-for-dollar funds from the federal government that match the amount they have raised through their own efforts. They can receive matching funds only if they agree to limit their spending to $37 million during the primaries.

Media: Press coverage of political events that communicate political issues and occurrences to the public. This coverage can be slanted in favor of a particular candidate.

National Conventions: National party conventions are huge media events where thousands of delegates convene to officially nominate their party's candidate. The convention provides a platform to declare their party's nominee and vice presidential running mate. The party platform is also discussed and announced at conventions.

Nominee: A person proposed by others for election to office.

Non-partisan: One who does not identify with any particular political party.

Partisan: A person strongly devoted to a political party.

Party: A group united by similar political values, joined to influence the election.

Platform: A statement of issues announced at party conventions.

Political Action Committee (PAC): Groups of people joined by a shared interest. A PAC can donate up to $5,000 per candidate per election.

Poll: The place where votes are cast. The term 'poll' is also used to describe a survey researching public opinion.

Pollster: A person or company whose duty is to research public opinion.

Precinct: The precinct is the smallest geographic unit in politics, dividing voters by neighborhood. A precinct can have between 200 and 1,000 voters.

Primaries: A stage in the election process in which voters cast their ballots for their preferred candidate or a delegate who represents that candidate. Primaries are the main way to nominate a candidate.

Rhetoric: The ability to effectively use language, through the practice of exaggeration or display, to influence others.

Running Mate: A presidential candidate will choose another individual to run for vice-president. This person is the president's running mate.

Soft Money: Funds raised by political parties directed towards party building and not directly towards supporting federal candidates.

Spin: The presentation of information that is biased or slanted to favor the candidates. Advisors to the candidates may engage in 'spin' in their communications to the media.

Straw Poll: A non-official, non-scientific study of voter preferences in a presidential election.

Suffrage: The right to vote.

Super Tuesday: a day in March when many states hold their primary elections at the same time.

Voting Methods: The mechanisms commonly used to cast a vote at a poll.

> **Paper** (rare, except for absentee votes)
>
> **Lever** (pulling a bar)
>
> **Optical scan** (filling in ovals on a paper with a pencil that is scanned by a special machine)
>
> **Punch card**: use puncher to punch hole next to the candidate's name
>
> **Direct Recording Electronic ("Touch Screen")**: Touch a button or a name on a monitor to record vote

Source: Based on C-SPAN's Glossary found at C-SPAN in the Classroom.

Presidential Debate – A discussion between presidential candidates held to address issues and campaign platforms. The first televised debate was held September 26, 1960 between John F. Kennedy and Richard Nixon. Evaluate the poster shown, using Clues to Understanding Photos on page 51.

"THE FIGHT OF THE YEAR"
ANYTHING CAN HAPPEN IN THIS BATTLE OF PUNCHES!

DICKIE
NIXON

"THE WHITTIER FLASH"

- VS. -

"CHECKERS' DADDY"

JACKIE
KENNEDY

"THE CAPE COD WHIZ"

"GREENBACK JACK"

65,000,000 ROUNDS

EXTRA ADDED ATTRACTION

H. C.   L. B. "ALAMO KID"
LODGE   VS.   JOHNSON
"THE BACK BAY BABY"   "LADY BIRD'S BOY"

TUES. NITE NOV. 8 · 7:00 P.M.
BILL WATTERS STADIUM
1271 ST. IVES PLACE, LOS ANGELES

TICKETS AVAILABLE - NO ADMISSION - THIS NITE ONLY
For Reservations: Call BRadshaw 2-0148

Research Activities/Things to Do

- It wasn't until 1947 that Miguel Trijillo, a Native American, won the suit that requires New Mexico and Arizona to allow suffrage for the people we took the land away from in those states (and elsewhere). Do some research in books, newspapers, or the internet to find out what this was all about.

- In 1961, the 23rd Amendment to the Constitution allowed residents of the District of Columbia to vote for President and Vice-President. Until this amendment, residents were unable to vote since the District is not a state. Why do you think people from the District had not been allowed to vote for other reasons? Explain your answer.

- Divide the class into ten groups, based on the groups you've written on the blackboard:

A = white women	B = minority women
C = white men	D = minority men
E = people 18-20 years old	F = men over 21 with property
G = illiterate men and women	H = non-citizens
I = resident of the D.C.	J = white men with no property

  Go back in time through U. S. history, and have a vote taken on various issues, such as the election for the 3rd president of the U. S., or Congress in 1840 or 1920. Only count the votes of the groups who were allowed to vote at that time in history. Have students identify when their group became enfranchised. Which group was the last to be enfranchised? Which group is still not allowed to vote? Then take a vote on an issue important to the students today, but place it at an earlier time in history.

  Example: Students under the age of 16 may not wear makeup or hats of any kind to school. The time of the vote is 1904. Whose votes will be counted? How does it feel not to be able to vote?

- Look up the results from the most recent Congressional election in your state. Which party won the most seats? How many incumbents won in their districts? How many women won? What can you conclude about your state's political profile? What percent of the registered voters actually voted? What can you do to encourage people to vote?

Clues to Understanding Photos and Graphics

Some or all of the following will help you to understand the photos in this book. Use a worksheet to jot down notes about the picture you are looking at. You may find this page helpful when looking at other photographs and graphics, too.

1. **What is the subject matter?**

2. **What details provide clues? Check each box that applies to the picture you are studying.**
   ☐ scene   ☐ buildings   ☐ people
   ☐ clothing   ☐ artifacts   ☐ time of day
   ☐ season   ☐ written message   ☐ activity
   ☐ other_____

3. **Can you tell where the picture was taken or illustration made?**

4. **What is the date? If there is no date, can you guess when it was probably taken or illustrated?**

5. **What is the purpose of the photo or graphic?**
   ☐ private use (family and friends)   ☐ recording an event
   ☐ for a news story   ☐ art
   ☐ advertising   ☐ education
   ☐ other_____

6. **Can you tell anything about the point of view of the graphic?**
   ☐ social or political *(is there is a message for the person looking at the photo)*
   ☐ sales tool *(someone is trying to sell something, a product or an idea)*
   ☐ educational *(the viewer is supposed to learn something from this)*

7. **What details make this photo or illustration interesting?**

8. **What can you learn about the people who lived at this time or in this place?**

Other Titles from
Discovery Enterprises, Ltd.

Researching American History

The following books include primary source documents with summaries of content, vocabulary, suggestions for analysis and research, and documents for practicing DBQ skills: (Ages 9-15 and to adult for readers of English as a second language)

America's Founders	*Northern Migration and*
A Century of Westward Expansion	*The Harlem Renaissance*
Children at Work	*The Orphan Trains*
The Civil War	*Reconstruction*
The Colonies	*The Revolutionary War*
The Constitution and The Bill of Rights	*Slavery*
The Declaration of Independence	*Spanish Explorers*
The Great Depression	*Transportation Stories*
Immigration	*Voting in America*
The Indian Wars	*Woman's Suffrage*
A Nation of Inventors	*World War I*
Native Americans	*World War II*

Perspectives on History Series

Seventy-five concise anthologies on focused topics in American history including written and graphic primary source documents. Each book contains 25 to 30 excerpts from primary source documents, one journal entry or letter written by a teenager who lived at the time, and a short excerpt from a classic piece of literature from or about the period. Books may be purchased individually or in boxed sets. Two educators' guides, based on this series, with practice DBQs are also available. (Ages 12 to adult)

Get A Clue!

An Introduction to Primary Sources and DBQs for young readers (ages 7-10)

Reproducible Plays on U. S. History topics

Twenty-four plays for classroom reading or performance, all on events in American History. May be purchased individually or in a set of all 24 plays. (Ages 10-15)

Contact for catalogs or information:

Discovery Enterprises, Ltd., 31 Laurelwood Dr., Carlisle, MA 01741
phone: 978-287-5401 fax: 978-287-5402 website: www.ushistorydocs.com